Lyver Pejadow rag Kenyver Jorna

Cornish Daily Prayer

Compiled by
Andy Phillips

Kernowek gans
Nicholas Williams

evertype

2009

Published by:
Dyllys gans:
Evertype, Cnoc Sceichín, Leac an Anfa, Cathair na Mart, Co. Mhaigh
Eo, Éire / Wordhen. *www.evertype.com.*

Second edition 2009.
Secùnd dyllans 2009.

A catalogue record for this book is available from the British Library.
Y kefyr covath rolyans rag an lyver-ma dhyworth an Lyverva Vretennek.

ISBN-10 1-904808-27-1
ISBN-13 978-1-904808-27-5

Typesetting, design, and cover by Michael Everson.
Set in Warnock Pro and Colmcille.
Olsettyans, desynyeth, ha cudhlen gans Michael Everson.
Olsettys in Warnock Pro ha Colmcille.

Printed by LightningSource.
Pryntys gans LightningSource.

Table of Contents

How to use this book

There are a great many people now seeking to learn Cornish, and all are looking for ways to use it in their daily lives. One is through the age-old practice of daily prayer. This book has been compiled with two aims—to help you to learn Cornish, and to bring you closer to God in the process.

Morning and Evening Prayer in this book follow a traditional format, and ancient prayers from the Celtic Church have been included whenever possible. A fixed psalm for Morning and Evening Prayer is used each day to make things simple, because that's how prayer should be. Collects have been included for use during the Church year, as well as a list of Celtic saints' days.

As for daily readings of scripture, the Cornish in this prayer book is Kernowek Standard (KS or 'Standard Cornish'). This is slightly different from the spelling used in the *Testament Noweth* (*New Testament*) translated by Professor Nicholas Williams and published in 2002. The differences between the two orthographies are, however, not great. It is suggested you merely start at the beginning of this, with Matthew's Gospel, reading 8 to 10 verses each morning and evening, until you have gone right through the New Testament. You might want to write a commentary as you go through so you do not need to keep thumbing through a dictionary or grammar when you return to it a second time. You will find the *Revised Standard Version* of the Bible is the most faithful translation if you want to refer to the text in English.

If you are starting to learn Cornish, you might begin using this prayer book by using mostly English, and then do a little more in Cornish each week or month, until you pray the whole of Morning or Evening Prayer in Cornish. If you wish to pray with others, one person can read out the prayers and the odd numbered verses of the canticles and psalms, the others just read out the even numbers of them. You might even use this book to start regular prayers in Cornish at your local church or chapel, perhaps for the first time in many, many years.

Eventually, you may find the psalms and Bible reading rather repetitious. The whole Bible in Cornish should be available soon; when it is, you might go to a church bookshop and buy a yearly schedule of holy days, readings and psalms (a lectionary) for the Church Year. You will know then that you have advanced greatly in understanding Cornish, and this little book's first aim will have been achieved.

As for the second, we can only hope and pray that you do indeed find in these pages a source of strength and peace, and come to know the living God who loves and sustains us all. To Him be praise and honour, glory and might, now and forever. *Amen.*

Bedneth Crist re bo genes,
    Andy Phillips
    Cowethas Peran Sans

Lyver Pejadow
rag Kenyver Jorna

Cornish Daily Prayer

Morning Prayer

Lord, who made land and sea, always be my aid,
And guide my life here in the way of truth.
Lord Jesus, look on me, and grant me your unfailing grace,
I seek, Lord Jesus, every hour in this life to please you.

Prayer of St Meriasek

Penitence

God the Father, have mercy on me.
God the Son, have mercy on me.
God the Holy Spirit, have mercy on me.
Blessed Trinity, holy and glorious, have mercy on me.

Almighty God, have mercy upon me,
forgive me my sins,
and lead me in life eternal. *Amen.*

Pejadow Myttyn

Arlùth, a wrug mor ha tir, pùb eur oll re'm weresso,
Ha roy dhybm i'n fordh a wir ow bêwnans obma gedya.
Jesu Arlùth, orthyf mir, ha'th lel grâss dhybmo grauntya.
Jesu, pùb eur oll ow desir yw i'n bÿs-ma dha blesya.

Pejadow Meryasek

Penytens

A Dhuw an Tas, kebmer mercy ahanaf.
A Dhuw an Mab, kebmer mercy ahanaf.
A Dhuw an Spyrys Sans, kebmer mercy ahanaf.
A Drynsys venegys, sans ha gloryes, kebmer mercy ahanaf.

Re gemerro Duw Ollgalosek mercy ahanaf,
re wrello gava dhybm ow fehosow
ha'm ledya bys i'n bêwnans eternal. Amen.

Venite *Psalm 95:1-7; 96:12b-13*

1   Come, let us sing to the Lord;
    let us shout for joy to the rock of our salvation.

2   Let us come before his presence with thanksgiving,
    and cry out to him joyfully in psalms.

3   For the Lord is a great God,
    and a great king above all gods.

4   In his hands are the depths of the earth,
    and the heights of the hills are his also.

5   The sea is his, for he made it,
    and his hands moulded the dry land.

6   Come, let us bow down and bend the knee,
    and kneel before the Lord our Maker.

7   For he is our God;
    we are the people of his pasture
    and the sheep of his hand.

8   O that today you would hearken to his voice,
    for he comes to judge the earth.

9   He will judge the world with righteousness
    and the peoples with his truth.

Venite *Salm 95:1-7; Salm 96:12b-13*

1   Deun, gwren ny cana dhe'n Arlùth;
    ha bedhen lowen yn colodnek in crefter agan sylwans.

2   Gesowgh ny dhe dhos dhyragtho gans grassyans,
    ha dysqwedhes agan honen lowenek dredho dre
        salmow.

3   Rag Duw brâs yth yw an Arlùth,
    ha mytern bras a-ugh oll an dhuwow.

4   Yma downder an norvÿs in y dhorn ev,
    hag ev a'n jeves nerth an brynyow kefrÿs.

5   Ev a bew an mor rag ev a'n gwrug,
    ha'y dhewla ev a formyas an tir sëgh.

6   Deun, gesowgh ny dhe wordhya ha plegya,
    ha mos wàr bedn dewlin dhyrag an Arlùth a wrug
        agan formya.

7   Rag ev yw agan Duw ny,
    pobel y borva on ny ha deves y dhorn.

8   Dâ via dhywgh hedhyw goslowes orth y lev,
    rag yma va ow tos rag jùjya an bÿs.

9   Ev a vydn y jùjya der ewnder,
    ha poblow an bÿs der y wiryoneth.

Psalm for Mondays *Psalm 1*

1   Happy are they who have not walked
    in the counsel of the wicked,
    nor lingered in the way of sinners,
    nor sat in the seats of the scornful!

2   Their delight is in the law of the Lord,
    and they meditate on his law day and night.

3   They are like trees planted by streams of water,
    bearing fruit in due season,
    with leaves that do not wither;
    everything they do shall prosper.

4   It is not so with the wicked:
    they are like chaff which the wind blows away;

5   Therefore the wicked shall not stand upright when
      judgement comes,
    nor the sinner in the council of the righteous.

6   For the Lord knows the way of the righteous,
    but the way of the wicked is doomed.

Salm De Lun *Salm 1*

1   Benegys yw hedna na wrug kerdhes
    in cùssul an debeles,
    na wrug sewya fordhow an behadoryon,
    naneyl kemeres y se in mesk an dus leun a scorn!

2   Saw yma y dhelit in laha an Arlùth,
    hag adro dhe'n laha-na ev a vydn predery dëdh ha nos.

3   Ev yw kepar ha gwedhen yw plynsys ryb goverow a
        dhowr,
    usy ow provia y frût i'n seson ewn,
    ha ny wra gwedhra hy delyow;
    ha mir, pynag oll a wrella, ev a vydn spedya.

4   Saw an debeles, ny vedhons y indella;
    y yw kepar hag usyon a vëdh scùllys gans an gwyns.

5   Rag hedna ny wra an debeles sevel in termyn an
        brusyans,
    naneyl ny sev pehadoryon in cùntelles an re gwiryon.

6   Rag yma an Arlùth ow kemeres with a fordh an re
        gwiryon,
    saw fordh an dus dhydhuw a wra mones dhe goll.

Psalm for Tuesdays *Psalm 14*

1 The fool has said in his heart, 'There is no God.'
All are corrupt and commit abominable acts;
there is none who does any good.

2 The Lord looks down from heaven
upon us all,
to see if any is wise,
if anyone seeks after God.

3 Everyone has proved faithless; all alike have turned
bad;
there is none who does good; no, not one.

4 Have they no knowledge, all those evildoers
who eat up my people like bread
and do not call upon the Lord?

5 See how they tremble with fear,
because God is in the company of the righteous.

6 Their aim is to confound the plans of the afflicted,
but the Lord is their refuge.

7 O that Israel's deliverance would come out of Zion!
when the Lord restores the fortunes of his people,
Jacob will rejoice and Israel be glad.

Salm De Mergh *Salm 14*

1   An fol a leverys in y golon, "Nyns eus Duw vëth oll."
Pedrys yns y yn kettep pedn ha gul taclow uthyk a
  wrowns;
nyns eus onen a wra dâ.

2   Yma an Arlùth ow meras mes a nev
orth mab den wàr an norvÿs,
may halla va gweles yw den vëth fur,
eus den vëth ow whelas Duw.

3   Yth yns oll gyllys mes a fordh; yth yns heb profyt.
Nyns eus onen a wra dâ — nag eus udn onen.

4   A ny wodhons y tra vëth, oll an drog-pobel-na,
usy ow tevorya ow fobel kepar ha bara
ha na wra pesy dhe'n Arlùth?

5   Mir, fatell usons y ow crena gans own brâs,
rag yma Duw in company an dus wiryon.

6   Porposys yns dhe ancombra towlow an den bohosek,
saw yth yw an Arlùth y dhefens.

7   A, re dheffo lyfreson Israel mes a Sion!
Pan wrella an Arlùth astevery fortyn y bobel,
ena Jacob a wra rejoycya, ha lowenek vëdh Israel.

Psalm for Wednesdays *Psalm 8*

1   O Lord our governor,
    how exalted is your name in all the world!

2   Out of the mouths of infants and children
    your majesty is praised above the heavens.

3   You have set up a stronghold against your adversaries,
    to quell the enemy and the avenger.

4   When I consider your heavens, the work of your
        fingers,
    the moon and the stars you have set in their courses,

5   What are mortals, that you should be mindful of
        them?
    mere human beings, that you should seek them out?

6   You have made them little lower than the angels;
    you adorn them with glory and honour.

7   You give them mastery over the works of your hands;
    and put all things under their feet,

8   All sheep and oxen,
    even the wild beasts of the field,

9   The birds of the air, the fish of the sea,
    and whatsoever walks in the paths of the sea.

10 O Lord our governor,
    how exalted is your name in all the world!

Salm De Merher *Salm 8*

1 A Arlùth, agan Governour,
    ass yw gloryes dha hanow in oll an bÿs!

2 Yma dha vrâster a-ugh an nevow ha whath y fëdh
      acowntys
    dre ganow babiow ha'n re munys ow tena.

3 Defens crev te re fùndyas warbydn oll dha eskerens,
    rag dyswul an enmy ha'n dialor.

4 Pàn esof ow consydra dha nevow, oberow dha vesyas,
    an loor ha'n stergan a wrusta gorra in ordyr,

5 Pandr'yw mebyon tus may festa prederus anodhans,
    bò mab den may whrelles kemeres with anodho?

6 Saw te re'n gwrug nebes isella ès an eleth,
    ha te re'n cùrunas gans glory hag onour.

7 Te re'n gwrug mêster a'th creacyon,
    ha re wrug kenyver tra sojeta dhodho in dadn y dreys,

8 Oll an deves ha'n ohen,
    hag oll bestas a'n gwel,

9 Ÿdhyn an air ha pùscas an mor,
    ha kenyver tra usy ow qwaya in fordhow an dowrow
      brâs.

10 A Arlùth, agan Governour,
    ass yw gloryes dha hanow in oll an bÿs!

Psalm for Thursdays *Psalm 100*

1 Be joyful in the Lord, all you lands;
   serve the Lord with gladness
   and come before his presence with a song.

2 Know this: The Lord himself is God;
   he himself has made us and we are his;
   we are his people and the sheep of his pasture.

3 Enter his gates with thanksgiving;
   go into his courts with praise;
   give thanks to him and call upon his name.

4 For the Lord is good; his mercy is everlasting;
   and his faithfulness endures from age to age.

Psalm for Fridays *Psalm 103*

1 Bless the Lord, O my soul,
   and all that is within me, bless his holy name.

2 Bless the Lord, O my soul,
   and forget not all his benefits.

3 He forgives all your sins
   and heals all your infirmities;

4 He redeems your life from the grave
   and crowns you with mercy and loving-kindness;

Salm De Yow *Salm 100*

1   Kenowgh dhe'n Arlùth gans ganow lowen,
    oll why pobel tregys wàr an nor;
    servyowgh an Arlùth gans lowender
    ha dewgh why dhyragtho gans cânow a joy

2   Godhvedhowgh an Arlùth fatell ywa Duw;
    ev a wrug agan gul, y bobel ev yth on ny;
    ny yw y dus ev ha deves y borva.

3   Dewgh aberth in y dharasow gans meur a wordhyans
    hag entrowgh in y gortys gans prais;
    rewgh grassys dhodho ha benegowgh y hanow sans.

4   Rag an Arlùth yw pòr dhâ; y gerensa yw sur rag nefra;
    yma y wiryoneth ow sevel crev dhyworth heneth dhe
       heneth.

Salm De Gwener *Salm 103*

1   Gwra benega an Arlùth, a enef dhybm,
    ha kebmys a vo inof, gwrêns benega y hanow sans.

2   Benyk an Arlùth, a enef dhybm,
    ha na wra ankevy oll y dhader.

3   Yma va ow cava dhis oll dha gabmweyth,
    hag ow sawya oll dha gleves.

4   Yma va ow sylwel dha enef dhyworth an bedh,
    hag orth dha gùruna gans mercy ha tregereth.

5 He satisfies you with good things,
and your youth is renewed like an eagle's.

6 The Lord executes righteousness
and judgement for all who are oppressed.

7 He made his ways known to Moses
and his works to the children of Israel.

8 The Lord is full of compassion and mercy,
slow to anger and of great kindness.

9 He will not always accuse us,
nor will he keep his anger for ever.

10 He has not dealt with us according to our sins,
nor rewarded us according to our wickedness.

11 For as the heavens are high above the earth,
so is his mercy great upon those who fear him.

12 As far as the east is from the west,
so far has he removed our sins from us.

Psalm for Saturdays *Psalm 65*

1 You are to be praised, O God, in Zion;
to you shall vows be performed who hear our prayer.

2 To you shall all flesh come,
because of their transgressions.

5 Yma va ow lenwel dha anow a daclow dâ,
   may fo nowedhys dha yowynkneth kepar hag er.

6 An Arlùth a wra ewnder,
   ha brusyans compes rag pynag oll a vo compressys.

7 Ev a dherivas y fordhow dhe Moyses,
   ha'y obereth dhe vebyon Israel.

8 Grassyes ha truethek yw an Arlùth;
   lent yw y sorr, mes y garadewder yw pòr vrâs.

9 Ny wra y acûsyans pesya benary,
   naneyl ny wra va sensy y sorr rag nefra.

10 Ny wrug ev dhyn warlergh agan pehosow,
   nag attylly dhyn warlergh agan drog-oberow.

11 Yn sur mar uhel del eus an ebron a-uhon,
   mar vrâs yw y gerensa lel tro ha'n re-na usy orth y gara.

12 Mar bell del yw an Ëst dhyworth an West,
   mar bell ev a wrug gorra dhyworthyn oll agan
   cabmweyth.

Salm De Sadorn *Salm 65*

1 Res yw dha braisya in Sion, a Dhuw;
   ha ny a goodh gul ambosow dhis usy ow clôwes agan
   pejadow.

2 Y teu pùb kig oll bys dhis,
   rag meneges aga fehosow;

3 Our sins are stronger than we are,
but you will blot them out.

4 Happy are they whom you choose
and draw to your courts to dwell there!
We will be satisfied by the beauty of your house,
by the holiness of your temple.

5 Awesome things will you show us in your
    righteousness,
O God of our salvation,
O hope of all the ends of the earth
and of the seas that are far away.

6 You make fast the mountains by your power;
they are girded about with might.

7 You still the roaring of the seas,
the roaring of their waves,
and the clamour of the peoples.

8 Those who dwell at the ends of the earth
will tremble at your marvellous signs;
you make the dawn and the dusk to sing for joy.

9 You take care of the earth
and shower it with water;
you make it rich and full of produce;
the river of God is full of water.

10 You prepare the grain,
for so you provide for the earth.

3 Pan wra agan drog-oberow prevailya wàr agan pydn,
   te a vydn aga fùrjya dhe ves.

4 Benegys yw hedna esta ow têwys hag ow kemeres
   dhis dha honen may halla va bos tregys genes i'th
      cortys;
   ny a vëdh lenwys a daclow dâ dha jy,
   taclow dha dempla sans.

5 Der oberow uthek te a vydn agan gortheby i'th ewnder,
   A Dhuw agan savyour;
   ha te yw govenek a oll pednow an bÿs
   hag a'n morow abell.

6 Dre dha nerth te a wrug fastya an menydhyow;
   hag yma oll power ha nerth i'th kerhyn.

7 Te a wrug spavenhe sorr brâs an mor
   ha'n todnow pan esens owth uja;
   te a wrug coselhe tervans oll an poblow.

8 An re-na usy tregys in pednow an bÿs,
   y a's teves own a'th varthùjyon;
   yma terry an jëdh ha'n gordhuwher orth dha braisya
      pùpprës.

9 Yth esta ow kemeres with a'n dor
   hag ow tevera dowr warnodho;
   te a'n gwra rych ha leun a drevas.
   leun a dhowr yw an ryver a Dhuw;

10 Pan esta ow provia rag an dor,
   te a dhora in rag ÿs rag mebyon tus.

17

11 You drench the furrows
   and smooth out the ridges;
   with heavy rain you soften the ground
   and bless its increase.

12 You crown the year with your goodness,
   and your paths overflow with plenty.

13 May the fields of the wilderness be rich for grazing,
   and the hills be clothed with joy.

14 May the meadows cover themselves with flocks
   and the valleys cloak themselves with grain;
   let them shout for joy and sing.

Psalm for Sundays *Psalm 148*

1 Alleluia! Praise the Lord from the heavens;
   praise him in the heights.

2 Praise him, all you angels of his;
   praise him, all his host.

3 Praise him, sun and moon;
   praise him, all you shining stars.

4 Praise him, heaven of heavens,
   and you waters above the heavens.

5 Let them praise the name of the Lord;
   for he commanded and they were created.

11 Yth esta ow clybya y fynglow
    hag ow levenhe an crybow yntredhans;
    yth esos orth y wul medhel gans glaw;
    benega a wreth y devyans avar.

12 An vledhen te a's cùrun gans dha dhader;
    ha'n trolerhow may whrusta kerdhes a vêdh ow
        tevera berry.

13 Y fêdh porva an gwylfos ow fedna;
    hag y fêdh lowena wàr an brynyow oll adro.

14 Yma an prasow gwyskys gans deves;
    hag y fêdh mar dew ŷs an nansow,
    may whrellons garma ha cana rag ewn lowena.

Salm De Sul *Salm 148*

1 Allelùya! Praisyowgh an Arlùth mes a nev;
    A, praisyowgh ev i'n uhelder.

2 Praisyowgh ev, oll why y eleth;
    A, praisyowgh ev, oll why y ostys.

3 Praisyowgh ev, why howl ha loor;
    praisyowgh ev, why y ster.

4 Praisyowgh ev, why nevow uhella,
    ha why, an dowrow usy a-ugh an nevow.

5 Gwrêns y oll praisya hanow an Arlùth;
    rag ev a gomondyas hag y a veu gwrês.

6 He made them stand fast for ever and ever;
  he gave them a law which shall not pass away.

7 Praise the Lord from the earth,
  you sea-monsters and all deeps;

8 Fire and hail, snow and fog,
  tempestuous wind, doing his will;

9 Mountains and all hills,
  fruit trees and all cedars;

10 Wild beasts and all cattle,
  creeping things and winged birds;

11 Kings of the earth and all peoples,
  princes and all rulers of the world;

12 Young men and maidens,
  old and young together.

13 Let them praise the name of the Lord,
  for his name only is exalted,
  his splendour is over earth and heaven.

14 He has raised up strength for his people
  and praise for all his loyal servants,
  the children of Israel, a people who are near him.
  Alleluia!

6 Ev a wrug aga fastya bys vycken;
  ev a wrug comondment na vëdh nefra bos defendys
    dhe ves.

7 A, praisyowgh an Arlùth dhyworth an nor;
  why uthvilas an mor ha whywhy, dowrow down brâs,

8 luhesen ha keser, nywl hag ergh,
  ha hager-awellow eus ow cuthyl warlergh y arhadɔw;

9 menydhyow hag oll why brynyow;
  gwëdh a dheg frût ha pùb cederen;

10 bestas gwyls hag oll gwarthek,
   taclow eus ow cramyas hag ÿdhyn askellek;

11 myterneth an bÿs hag oll poblow;
   pryncys ha rewlysy oll an bÿs;

12 tus yonk ha meghtythyon,
   tus coth ha flehes warbarth.

13 Gwrêns y oll gormola hanow an Arlùth;
   rag ny vëdh exaltys saw unsel y hanow ev.
   Uhella yw y wordhyans ès an norvÿs ha'n nev.

14 Ev re dhrehevys in bàn corn y bobel;
   rag hedna ev a vëdh praisys gans oll y wesyon;
   gans flehes Israel, pobel usy ogas dhodho.
   Allelùya!

Reading of Scripture

Silence

Benedictus *Luke 1:68-79*

1   Blessed be the Lord the God of Israel:
    for he has come to his people and set them free.

2   He has raised up for us a mighty Saviour:
    born of the house of his servant David.

3   Through his holy prophets he promised of old that he
        would save us from our enemies: from the hands of
        all that hate us.

4   He promised to show mercy to our forebears:
    and to remember his holy covenant.

5   This was the oath he swore to our father Abraham:
    to set us free from the hands of our enemies,

6   Free to worship him without fear:
    holy and righteous in his sight all the days of our life.

7   You my child shall be called the prophet of the Most
        High:
    for you will go before the Lord to prepare his way.

8   To give his people knowledge of salvation:
    by the forgiveness of all their sins.

Redyans mes a'n Scryptùr

Taw

Benedictùs *Lûk 1:68-79*

1   Benegys re bo Arlùth Duw Israel:
    rag ev re vysytyas y bobel ha'ga dasprena.

2   Hag ev re dhrehevys ragon Savyour brâs:
    genys a jy y servont Davyth.

3   Ev a dhedhewys i'n dedhyow coth wàr anow y brofusy
    sans: y whre va agan sylwel dhyworth agan envy ha
    mes a dhewla oll agan eskerens.

4   Ev a bromysyas dhe gemeres trueth a'gan tasow:
    ha dhe remembra y ambos sans.

5   Hèm o an ty a dos ev dhe Abraham agan tas:
    y fydna agan delyvra mes a dhewla agan envy,

6   may fen ny frank dh'y wordhya heb own:
    in ewnder hag in sansoleth oll dedhyow agan bêwnans.

7   Te, ow flogh, a vëdh gelwys profus an Duw Uhella:
    drefen te dhe gerdhes dhyragtho ha parusy y fordh,

8   may halles ry dh'y bobel godhvos a salvacyon:
    rag may fe gyvys oll aga fehosow.

9   In the tender compassion of our God:
    the dawn from on high shall break upon us,

10 To shine on those who dwell in darkness
    and the shadow of death:
    and to guide our feet into the way of peace.

The Collect

*Collects for saints' days and for times of the Church year
are to be found in the relevant section. If none are
appropriate, the following is used:*

Lord, be with us this day,
Within us to purify us;
Above us to draw us up;
Beneath us to sustain us;
Before us to lead us;
Behind us to restrain us;
Around us to protect us.

St Patrick

9 In tregereth hegar agan Duw:
   terry an jëdh a vydn dos warnan dhia nev avàn,

10 may halla golowy an re-na esa tregys in tewolgow
   hag i'n skeus a vernans:
   ha gedya agan treys i'n fordhow a gosoleth.

An Collect

*Y kefyr collectys rag sesons a vledhen an Eglos i'n radn ewn
awoles. Mar ny vydn servya onen vëth anodhans, y fëdh
ûsys onen a'n collectys-ma a sew:*

Re bo an Arlùth genen hedhyw,
Inon ny rag agan pùryfia;
A-uhon rag agan tedna in bàn;
In dadnon rag agan sensy;
Dhyragon rag agan gedya;
Adrëv dhyn rag agan lettya;
Adro dhyn rag agan defendya.

Padryk Sans

The Lord's Prayer

Our Father, who art in heaven,
hallowed be thy name.
Thy kingdom come,
thy will be done,
on earth as it is in heaven.
Give us this day our daily bread,
and forgive us our trespasses,
as we forgive them who trespass against us.
And lead us not into temptation,
but deliver us from evil.
For thine is the kingdom, the power and the glory,
forever and ever. *Amen.*

Private intercessions may be made here

The grace of our Lord Jesus Christ, and the love of God,
and the fellowship of the Holy Spirit
be with us all now and for evermore. *Amen.*

An Pader

Agan Tas ny, eus in nev,
benegys re bo dha hanow.
Re dheffo dha wlascor,
dha vodh re bo gwrës
i'n nor kepar hag in nev.
Ro dhyn hedhyw agan bara a bùb dëdh oll
ha gav dhyn agan cabmweyth,
kepar dell eson ny ow gava dhe'n re-na usy ow cul
      cabmweyth wàr agan pydn ny.
Ha na wra agan gorra in temptacyon,
mès delyrf ny dhyworth drog.
Rag dhyso y yw an wlascor, ha'n gallos ha'n gordhvans,
bys vycken ha bys venary. *Amen.*

Y hyllyr gul pejadow pryveth obma.

Grâss agan Arlùth Jesu Crist, kerensa Duw,
ha cowethyans an Spyrys Sans
re bo genen ny oll bys vycken ha bys venary. *Amen.*

27

Evening Prayer

The power and comfort of the Father be always with us;
Jesus the Son, full of grace, aid us night and day;
The blessed Holy Spirit, its grace to us supply;
Mary, Mother and Virgin, for God's mercy, pray for us.

Prayer of St Sylvester

Penitence

God the Father, have mercy on me.
God the Son, have mercy on me.
God the Holy Spirit, have mercy on me.
Blessed Trinity, holy and glorious, have mercy on me.

Almighty God, have mercy upon me,
forgive me my sins,
and lead me in life eternal. *Amen.*

Pejadow Gordhuwher

Gallos ha confort an Tas re bo genen pùb termyn;
Jesu, an Mab leun a ras, socor ny mo ha myttyn;
An Spyrys Sans benegys y râss genen may kyffyn;
Maria, Mabm ha Gwerhes, dhe vercy Duw pÿs ragon.

Pejadow Sen Sylvester

Penytens

A Dhuw an Tas, kebmer mercy ahanaf.
A Dhuw an Mab, kebmer mercy ahanaf.
A Dhuw an Spyrys Sans, kebmer mercy ahanaf.
A Drynsys benegys, sans ha gloryes, kebmer mercy
     ahanaf.

Re gemerro Duw Ollgalosek mercy ahanaf,
re wrello gava dhym ow fehosow
ha'm ledya bys i'n bêwnans eternal. *Amen.*

The Opening Psalm *Psalm 67*

1 May God be merciful to us and bless us,
show us the light of his countenance and come to us.

2 Let your ways be known upon earth,
your saving health among all nations.

3 Let the peoples praise you, O God;
let all the peoples praise you.

4 Let the nations be glad and sing for joy,
for you judge the peoples with equity
and guide all the nations upon earth.

5 Let the peoples praise you, O God;
let all the peoples praise you.

6 The earth has brought forth her increase;
may God, our own God, give us his blessing.

7 May God give us his blessing,
and may all the ends of the earth stand in awe of him.

An Salm Wostalleth *Salm 67*

1   Re bo Duw grassyes dhyn ny ha'gan benega,
    ha gul dh'y fâss dewynya warnan.

2   Bedhens dha fordhow aswonys i'n norvÿs,
    ha'th power a sylwans in mesk oll an nacyons.

3   Gwrêns oll an poblow dha braisya, a Dhuw,
    gwrêns oll an poblow dha braisya.

4   Bedhens an nacyons lowen ha gwrêns y cana,
    rag yth esta ow jùjya an poblow der ewnder
    ha te a wra gedya pùb nacyon a'n bÿs.

5   Gwrêns oll an poblow dha braisya, a Dhuw,
    gwrêns oll an poblow dha braisya.

6   I'n eur-na an dor a vydn dry in rag y drevas,
    ha Duw, agan Duw ny, a wra agan benega.

7   Duw a wra agan benega,
    ha pednow an bÿs a vydn kemeres own dhyragtho.

Psalm for Mondays *Psalm 121*

1   I lift up my eyes to the hills;
    from where is my help to come?

2   My help comes from the Lord,
    the maker of heaven and earth.

3   He will not let your foot be moved
    and he who watches over you will not fall asleep.

4   Behold, he who keeps watch over Israel
    shall neither slumber nor sleep;

5   The Lord himself watches over you;
    the Lord is your shade at your right hand,

6   So that the sun shall not strike you by day,
    nor the moon by night.

7   The Lord shall preserve you from all evil;
    it is he who shall keep you safe.

8   The Lord shall watch over your going out
    and your coming home,
    from this time forth for evermore.

Salm De Lun *Salm 121*

1 Me a vydn drehevel ow dewlagas dhe'n brynyow;
  saw pana dyller a vydn ow gweres dos dhyworto?

2 Ow gweres a vydn dos dhyworth an Arlùth,
  a wrug an nev ha'n nor.

3 Ny vydn ev gasa dha droos dhe vos gwayys,
  hag ev usy orth dha wetha, ny wra va codha in cùsk.

4 Mir, gwethyas Israel,
  ny wra va naneyl powes na cùsca.

5 An Arlùth y honen yw dha warden,
  yth yw an Arlùth dha skeus adhyhow dhis,

6 ma na wrella an howl dha bystyga orth golow dedh,
  naneyl an loor dha weskel i'n nos.

7 An Arlùth a wra dha wetha orth pùb drog;
  yth yw ev a wra sensy dha vêwnans.

8 An Arlùth a wra dha ventena pan wrylly mos
  ajy bò dos in mes,
  alebma rag bys vycken ha rag nefra.

Psalm for Tuesdays *Psalm 23*

1 The Lord is my shepherd;
   I shall not be in want.

2 He makes me lie down in green pastures
   and leads me beside still waters.

3 He revives my soul
   and guides me along right pathways for his name's
      sake.

4 Though I walk through the valley of the shadow of
      death,
   I shall fear no evil;
   for you are with me;
   your rod and your staff, they comfort me.

5 You spread a table before me
   in the presence of those who trouble me;
   you have anointed my head with oil,
   and my cup is running over.

6 Surely your goodness and mercy shall follow me
   all the days of my life,
   and I will dwell in the house of the Lord for ever.

Salm De Mergh *Salm 23*

1 An Arlùth yw ow bugel,
   ma na'm bëdh othem a dra vëth.

2 Ev a wra gul dhybm growedha in porva a wels gwer;
   ryb an dowrow cosel ev a vydn ow hùmbronk.

3 Ev a wra gul dhe'm enef dasvewa;
   ev a'm gorr in fordhow a wiryoneth rag kerensa y
      hanow ev.

4 Kyn whrellen kerdhes dre nans an skeus a ancow,
   me ny'm bëdh own a dhrog vëth oll,
   aban esta jy genama;
   dha welen ha'th vagyl a wra ow honfortya.

5 Te a vydn parusy tabel dhyragof
   in fâss an re-na usy orth ow throbla;
   gans oyl te a wra ùntya ow fedn
   ha'm hanaf a vëdh gorlenwys.

6 In gwir, dha dhader ha'th tregereth a wra ow sewya
   oll dedhyow ow bêwnans;
   ha me a vëdh tregys in chy an Arlùth bys venary.

35

Psalm for Wednesdays *Psalm 46*

1   God is our refuge and strength,
    a very present help in trouble;

2   Therefore we will not fear, though the earth be
        moved,
    and though the mountains be toppled
    into the depths of the sea;

3   Though its waters rage and foam,
    and though the mountains tremble at its tumult.

4   The Lord of hosts is with us;
    the God of Jacob is our stronghold.

5   There is a river whose streams
    make glad the city of God;
    the holy habitation of the Most High.

6   God is in the midst of her; she shall not be
        overthrown;
    God shall help her at the break of day.

7   The nations make much ado
    and the kingdoms are shaken;
    God has spoken and the earth shall melt away.

8   The Lord of hosts is with us;
    the God of Jacob is our stronghold.

9   Come now and look upon the works of the Lord,
    what awesome things he has done on earth.

Salm De Merher *Salm 46*

1   Duw yw agan govenek ha'gan nerth;
    gweres pòr ogas ywa i'n termyn a bonvos.

2   Rag hedna ny vydnon ny perthy own, kyn fe muvys an
      nor;
    ha kyn fe an menydhyow dysevys
    ha tôwlys in downder an mor;

3   Kyn whrella y dhowrow serry ha drehevel fol;
    kyn whrella an menydhyow crena orth y dervans.

4   Yma an Arlùth a Luyow orth agan scodhya,
    hag yth yw Duw Jacob agan dinas crev.

5   Frosow an ryver
    a wra lowenhe cyta Duw;
    an tyller sans, scovva an Duw Uhella.

6   Yma Duw i'n cres anedhy; rag hedna ny vëdh hy
      gwayys;
    Duw a wra hy gweres orth terry an jëdh.

7   An nacyons a wra serry meur
    ha kenyver gwlascor a vëdh crehyllys;
    saw Duw re gowsas ha'n nor a vydn tedha ha mos dhe
      goll.

8   Yma an Arlùth a Luyow orth agan scodhya,
    hag yth yw Duw Jacob agan dinas crev.

9   Dewgh nes ha meras orth obereth an Arlùth;
    pana daclow uthek yw gwrës ganso wàr an norvÿs.

10 It is he who makes war to cease in all the world;
   he breaks the bow and shatters the spear
   and burns the shields with fire.

11 "Be still, then, and know
   that I am God;
   I will be exalted among the nations."

12 The Lord of hosts is with us;
   the God of Jacob is our stronghold.

Psalm for Thursdays *Psalm 91*

1 He who dwells in the shelter of the Most High,
   abides under the shadow of the Almighty.

2 He shall say to the Lord,
   "You are my refuge and my stronghold,
   my God in whom I put my trust."

3 He shall deliver you from the snare of the hunter
   and from the deadly pestilence.

4 He shall cover you with his pinions,
   and you shall find refuge under his wings;
   his faithfulness shall be a shield and buckler.

5 You shall not be afraid of any terror by night,
   nor of the arrow that flies by day;

6 Of the plague that stalks in the darkness,
   nor of the sickness that lays waste at midday.

10 Ev a vydn gul dhe werryans cessya in oll an bÿs;
   ev a vydn shyndya an warak ha terry an guw dhe
      dybmyn
   ha lesky an charettys dre dan.

11 "Rag hedna bedhowgh cosel ha godhvedhowgh
   ow bosaf Duw;
   me a vëdh exaltys in mesk an nacyons."

12 Yma an Arlùth a Luyow orth agan scodhya,
   hag yth yw Duw Jacob agan dinas crev.

Salm De Yow *Salm 91*

1 Pynag oll a vo tregys in goskes an Duw Uhella,
   hag a wrella gortos in dadn skeus Duw Ollgalosek,

2 Ev a vydn leverel dhe'n Arlùth,
   "Te yw ow harber ha'm dinas,
   an Duw mayth esof vy ow trestya ino."

3 Ev a wra dha dhelyvra mes a vaglen an helghyer,
   ha dhyworth plagys fell.

4 Der y eskelly ev a vydn dha gudha
   ha te a vëdh saw in dadn y bluv;
   y lendury a vëdh dha scoos ha'th tefens.

5 Ny wreta kemeres own a uth vëth y'n nos,
   nag a'n seth a vëdh ow neyja dëdhweyth;

6 Nag a'n pla usy ow kerdhes y'n tewolgow;
   nag a'n cleves a wra dystrewy dohajëdh.

7   A thousand shall fall at your side
    and ten thousand at your right hand,
    but it shall not come near you.

8   Your eyes have only to behold
    to see the reward of the wicked.

9   Because you have made the Lord your refuge,
    and the Most High your habitation.

10 There shall no evil happen to you,
    neither shall any plague come near your dwelling.

11 For he shall give his angels charge over you,
    to keep you in all your ways.

12 They shall bear you in their hands,
    lest you dash your foot against a stone.

13 You shall tread upon the lion and adder;
    you shall trample the young lion and the serpent
        under your feet.

14 Because he is bound to me in love,
    therefore will I deliver him;
    I will protect him,
    because he knows my name.

15 He shall call upon me and I will answer him;
    I am with him in trouble,
    I will rescue him and bring him to honour.

16 With long life will I satisfy him,
    and show him my salvation.

7 Mil a yll codha rybos
ha deg mil adhyhow dhis;
saw ny wra an pla dha dùchya jy.

8 Gans dha dhewlagas dha honen te a wra gweles;
ha meras orth reward an drog-bobel.

9 Yth yw an Arlùth y honen dha harber,
ha te re wrug dha dhinas a'n Duw Uhella.

10 Rag hedna ny wra drog vëth codha warnas;
naneyl ny wra dos plag vëth ogas dhe'th scovva.

11 Rag ev a vydn comondya y eleth,
dhe'th wetha in oll dha fordhow.

12 Y a vydn dha dhon in bàn,
rag dowt te dhe bystyga dha droos warbydn men.

13 Te a vydn trettya an lion ha'n nader;
an lion yonk ha'n serpont te a vydn trettya in dadn
dreys.

14 Dre reson y vos kelmys dhybm dre gerensa,
rag hedna me a vydn y dhelyvra;
me a vydn y dhrehevel in bàn mes a beryl,
drefen ev dhe aswon ow hanow vy.

15 Pan wrello gelwel warnaf, me a vydn y wortheby;
me a vëdh ganso in trobel,
me a vydn y sawya ha'y dhon dhe onour.

16 Me a vydn y gontentya dre vêwnans hir,
ha'y lenwel a'm salvacyon.

Psalm for Fridays *Psalm 4*

1 Answer me when I call, O God,
  defender of my cause;
  you set me free when I am hard-pressed;
  have mercy on me and hear my prayer.

2 "You mortals, how long will you
  dishonour my glory;
  how long will you worship dumb idols
  and run after false gods?"

3 Know that the Lord
  does wonders for the faithful;
  when I call upon the Lord, he will hear me.

4 Tremble, then, and do not sin;
  upon your bed
  speak to your heart in silence.

5 Offer the appointed sacrifices;
  and put your trust in the Lord.

6 Many are saying,
  "O that we might see better times!'
  Lift up the light of your countenance upon us, O Lord."

7 You have put gladness in my heart, more than when
   grain, wine and oil increase.

8 I lie down in peace; at once I fall asleep;
  for only you, Lord, make me dwell in safety.

Salm De Gwener *Salm 4*

1 Gwra ow gortheby pan ven ow kelwel,
   a Dhuw ow gwiryoneth;
   pan vedhen compressys te a'm delyvras,
   bëdh grassyes dhym lebmyn ha goslow orth ow
       fejadow.

2 "A vebyon tus, pana bellder a vydnowgh why
   trailya oll ow glory dhe sham;
   pana bellder a vedhowgh why ow cara taclow cog
   hag ow whelas gowegneth?"

3 Godhvedhowgh fatell dhysquedhas an Arlùth dhybm
   y garadewder marthys;
   pan wryllyf gelwel, an Arlùth a vydn ow clôwes.

4 Gwra crena ha sevel orth pegh;
   gwra ombredery wàr dha wely
   i'th colon dha honen ha bëdh cosel.

5 Y res dhis offra an offrydnow a vo ewn;
   ha trestya i'n Arlùth.

6 Yma meur a dus ow leverel,
   "Pyw a vydn dysqwedhes dhyn dâ vëth?
   Golow dha fâss, a Arlùth, yw gyllys qwit dhyworthyn."

7 Saw te re ros moy lowender dhe'm colon; ès an re-na
       pan vo ÿs, gwin hag oyl owth encressya ragthans.

8 Me a vydn gorwedha in cres ha cùsca;
   rag te yn udnek, a Dhuw, a'm gwra trega gans sawment.

43

Psalm for Saturdays *Psalm 24*

1 The earth is the Lord's and all that is in it,
the world and all who dwell therein.

2 For it is he who founded it upon the seas
and made it firm upon the rivers of the deep.

3 "Who can ascend the hill of the Lord?
and who can stand in his holy place?"

4 "Those who have clean hands and a pure heart,
who have not pledged themselves to falsehood,
nor sworn by what is a fraud.

5 'They shall receive a blessing from the Lord
and a just reward from the God of their salvation."

6 Such is the generation of those who seek him,
of those who seek your face, O God of Jacob.

7 Lift up your heads, O gates;
lift them high, O everlasting doors;
and the King of glory shall come in.

8 "Who is this King of glory?"
"The Lord, strong and mighty, the Lord, mighty in
battle."

9 Lift up your heads, O gates;
lift them high, O everlasting doors;
and the King of glory shall come in.

10 "Who is he, this King of glory?"
"The Lord of hosts, he is the King of glory."

Salm De Sadorn *Salm 24*

1   Dhe'n Arlùth yma an nor ha pynag oll eus ino;
    an norvÿs oll ha'n re-na usy ino tregys.

2   Rag ev re'n growndyas wàr an morow,
    ha'y fùndya wàr an an lyvyow.

3   "Pyw a yll ascendya bys in meneth an Arlùth,
    ha pyw a wra sevel in y dyller sans?"

4   "Kenyver a vo glân y dhewla ha pur y golon,
    na wrug ambosa y honen dhe falsury
    na gowlia rag tùlla y gentrevak.

5   Ev a vydn receva bedneth dhyworth an Arlùth,
    ha gwirvreus dhyworth an Duw a'y salvacyon."

6   Indella yw heneth an re-na usy orth y whelas,
    an keth re-na usy ow whelas fâss an Duw a Jacob.

7   Drehevowgh agas pednow, why porthow,
    ha bedhowgh lyftys in bàn, why darasow coth;
    may halla dos ajy an Mytern a glory.

8   "Pyw yw an Mytern a glory?"
    "An Arlùth crev ha galosek, an Arlùth galosek in batel."

9   Drehevowgh agas pednow, why porthow,
    drehevowgh y in bàn kefrÿs, why darasow coth;
    ha'n Mytern a glory a vydn dos ajy.

10 "Pyw yw an Mytern a glory?"
    "An Arlùth a Luyow, ev yw an Mytern a glory."

45

Psalm for Sundays *Psalm 16*

1 Protect me, O God,
   for I take refuge in you;
   I have said to the Lord, 'You are my Lord,
   my good above all other.'

2 All my delight is upon the godly that are in the land,
   upon those who are noble among the people.

3 But those who run after other gods
   shall have their troubles multiplied.

4 Their libations of blood I will not offer,
   nor take the names of their gods upon my lips.

5 O Lord, you are my portion and my cup;
   it is you who uphold my lot.

6 My boundaries enclose a pleasant land;
   indeed, I have a goodly heritage.

7 I will bless the Lord who gives me counsel;
   my heart teaches me, night after night.

8 I have set the Lord always before me;
   because he is at my right hand I shall not fall.

9 My heart, therefore, is glad
   and my spirit rejoices;
   my body also shall rest in hope.

Salm De Sul *Salm 16*

1 Gwra ow gwetha vy, a Dhuw,
   rag inos jy me re gemeras harber;
   me re leverys dhe'n Arlùth "Te yw ow arlùth,
   ha genes jy yma ow powes oll ow les."

2 Yma oll ow delit wàr an dus sans usy i'n pow,
   wàr an re-na yw nobyl in mesk an bobel.

3 An re-na usy ow resek warlergh duwow erel,
   encressya a wra aga throblys.

4 Ny vanaf vy devera in mes goos-offrydnow dhedhans,
   naneyl ny wrama kemeres aga henwyn wàr ow
      gwessyow.

5 An Arlùth yw ow shara appoyntys ha'm hanaf vy;
   seker yw ow fortyn y'th tewla jy.

6 In tyller hegar yma an gevran yw codhys dhybm,
   hag ow fossessyon yma in tireth teg.

7 Me a vydn benega an Arlùth a ros dhym cùssul;
   i'n nos kefrÿs ev re dhescas ow holon.

8 An Arlùth me re'n settyas dhyragof pùpprës;
   yma va adhyhow dhybm ha ny wrama nefra fyllel.

9 Rag hedna lowenek yw ow holon
   hag ow spyrys yw leun a joy;
   hag ow hig inwedh a wra powes in sawment.

10 For you will not abandon me to the grave,
    nor let your holy one see the Pit.

11 You will show me the path of life;
    in your presence there is fullness of joy,
    and in your right hand are pleasures for evermore.

Reading of Scripture

Silence

Magnificat *Luke 1:46-55*

If it is very late in the evening, the Nunc Dimittis that follows is said instead.

1   My soul proclaims the greatness of the Lord:
    my spirit rejoices in God my Saviour;

2   For he has looked with favour on his lowly servant:
    from this day all generations will call me blessed.

3   The Almighty has done great things for me:
    and holy is his name.

4   He has mercy on those who fear him:
    in every generation.

5   He has shown the strength of his arm:
    he has scattered the proud in their conceit.

10 Rag ny vynta ow ry aberth i'n power a vernans,
  naneyl ny wreta alowa dha servont lel dhe weles
    podrethes.

11 Te a vydn dysqwedhes dhybm an fordh a vêwnans:
  i'th presens jy yma an leunder a joy,
    hag y fëdh whecter ow tevera mes a'th torn dyhow bys
      vycken.

Redyans mes a'n Scryptùr

Taw

Magnificat *Luk 1:46-55*

*Mar pëdh an termyn pòr adhewedhes i'n gordhuwher, in le
an Magnificat y fëdh leverys an Nunc Dimittis. Gweler
wosa hebma.*

1 Yma ow enef ow moghhe an Arlùth:
  ha'm spyrys re rejoycyas in Duw ow Savyour.

2 Rag ev re veras orth uvelder y vowes;
  hag alebma rag pùb heneth a'm gelow benegys.

3 Rag hedna neb yw galosek re wrug ow moghhe;
  ha sans yw y hanow ev.

4 Y vercy a vëdh wàr an re-na usy ow perthy own
    anodho,
  dhia heneth dhe heneth.

5 Ev re dhysqwedhas gallos der y vregh,
  ha scùllya an re gothys ales in desmyk aga holon.

49

6 He has cast down the mighty from their thrones:
   and has lifted up the lowly.

7 He has filled the hungry with good things:
   and the rich he has sent away empty.

8 He has come to the help of his servant Israel:
   for he has remembered his promise of mercy,

9 The promise he made to our forebears:
   to Abraham and his children for ever.

Nunc Dimittis *Luke 2:29-32*

1 Lord, now you let your servant rest in peace,
   your word has been fulfilled.

2 My own eyes have seen the salvation:
   which you have prepared in the sight of every people;

3 A light to reveal you to the nations:
   and the glory of your people Israel.

6 Ev re iselhas an vrâsyon dhywar aga se,
   hag exaltya an re uvel ha'n re clor.

7 Ev re lenwys an re nownek a daclow dâ,
   ha'n dus rych ev a's danvonas gwag in kerdh.

8 Ev a remembras y vercy
   ha socra y servont Israel,

9 kepar del wruga promysya dh'agan hendasow,
   dhe Abraham ha dh'y issyw bys vycken.

Nunc Dimittis *Luk 2:29-32*

1 I'n tor'-ma, a Arlùth, yth esos ow tanvon dha servont
   dhe ves in cosoleth; warlergh dha lavar.

2 Ow dewlagas ow honen re welas dha sylwans;
   a wrussys parusy dhyrag fâss oll an poblow,

3 May halla bos golow dhe wolowy an Jentylys,
   ha glory dhe'th pobel Israel.

The Collect

*Collects for saints days and for times of the Church year are
to be found in the relevant section. If none are appropriate,
the following is used:*

Grant, O God Thy protection,
And in protection, power,
And in power, wisdom,
And in wisdom, knowledge,
And in knowledge, knowledge of what is just,
And in knowledge of what is just, the love of it,
And from loving, to love all existence,
And in all existence to love God:
God and all goodness.

Prayer of the Cornish Gorsedd

An Collect

Y kefyr collectys rag sesons a vledhen an Eglos i'n radn ewn awoles. Mar ny vydn servya onen vëth anodhans, y fëdh ûsys an geryow-ma a sew:

Roy, a Dhuw, dha with
hag in gwith, nerth,
hag in nerth, skians,
hag i'n skians, godhvos,
hag i'n godhvos, godhvos an ewn,
hag i'n godhvos an ewn, y gara,
hag a gara, cara pùb bêwnans,
hag in pùb bêwnans cara Duw,
Duw ha pùb dader.

Pejadow Gorseth Kernow

The Lord's Prayer

Our Father, who art in heaven,
hallowed be thy name.
Thy kingdom come,
thy will be done,
on earth as it is in heaven.
Give us this day our daily bread,
and forgive us our trespasses,
as we forgive them who trespass against us.
And lead us not into temptation,
but deliver us from evil.
For thine is the kingdom, the power and the glory,
forever and ever. *Amen.*

Private intercessions may be made here

Keep me safe, Lord, in the darkness of this night,
for the eternal kingdom,
where there is flaming radiance for ever.
    Amen.

Early Irish Prayer

An Pader

Agan Tas ny, eus in nev,
benegys re bo dha hanow.
Re dheffo dha wlascor,
dha vodh re bo gwrës
i'n nor kepar hag in nev.
Ro dhyn hedhyw agan bara a bùb dëdh oll
ha gav dhyn agan cabmweyth,
kepar dell eson ny ow cava dhe'n re-na usy ow cul
 cabmweyth er agan pydn ny.
Ha na wra agan gorra in temptacyon,
mès delyrf ny dhyworth drog.
Rag dhyso jy yw an wlascor, ha'n gallos ha'n gordhyans,
bys vycken ha bys venary. *Amen.*

Y hyllyr gul pejadow pryveth omma.

Gwith vy saw, Arlùth, in tewolgow an nos-ma
rag an wlascor heb dyweth,
may fëdh golowys ow tewynya bys vycken ha bys venary.
 Amen.

Pejadow Godhalek Avar

Collects and Prayers

Collects

Advent

Almighty God, give us grace that we may cast away the works of darkness and put upon us the armour of light, now in the time of this mortal life, in which your Son Jesus Christ came to visit us in great humility; that in the last day, when he shall come again in his glorious majesty, to judge both the living and the dead, we may rise to the life immortal; through him who lives and reigns with you and the Holy Spirit, now and forever. *Amen.*

Christmas Day until Epiphany

Almighty God, who has given to us your only Son to take our nature upon him, and as at this time to be born of a pure virgin; grant that we being renewed, and made your children by adoption and grace, may daily be inspired by your Holy Spirit; through the same our Lord Jesus Christ, who lives and reigns with you and the same Spirit, ever one God, world without end. *Amen.*

Collectys ha Pejadow

Collectys

Asvens

A Dhuw Ollgalosek, graunt dhyn ny grâss dhe dôwlel dhywarnan oberow an tewlder ha gorra i'gan kerhyn hernes an golow, lebmyn in termyn an bêwnans mortal-ma, may whrug dha Vab Agan Arlùth Jesu Crist ino agan vysytya in uvelder bras; i'n jorna dewetha pàn dheffa va arta in y Vrâster gloryes dhe jùjya an re bew ha'n re marow, may hallen ny drehevel dhe'n bêwnans dyvarow; dredho ev usy ow rewlya yn few genes ha gans an Spyrys Sans trank heb worfen. *Amen.*

Dëdh Nadelek Bys in Degol Stool

A Dhuw Ollgalosek, te re ros dhyn dha Udn Vab dhe gemeres warnodho agan natur ha dhe vos genys avell y'n seson-ma a werhes pur, graunt dhyn bos daskenys dre adopcyon ha grâss may fen ny nowedhys kenyver jorna a'th Spyrys Sans; der an keth Jesu Crist agan Arlùth usy ow rewlya yn few genes ha gans an Spyrys Sans trank heb worfen. *Amen.*

Epiphany *6 January*
Eternal God, who by the shining of a star led the wise men to the worship of your Son: guide by his light the nations of the earth, that the whole world may behold your glory; through Jesus Christ our Lord. *Amen.*

Presentation of Christ in the Temple *2 February*
Almighty Father, whose Son Jesus Christ was presented in the Temple and acclaimed the glory of Israel and the light of the Gentiles, grant that in him we may be presented to you, and in the world may reflect his glory; through Jesus Christ our Lord. *Amen.*

The Annunciation *25 March*
We ask you, O Lord, to pour your grace into our hearts; that as we have know the incarnation of your Son Jesus Christ by the message of an angel, so by his cross and passion we may be brought to the glory of his resurrection; through Jesus Christ our Lord. *Amen.*

Ash Wednesday and Lent
Almighty God, whose Son Jesus Christ fasted forty days in the wilderness, and was tempted as we are, yet without sin: give us grace to discipline ourselves, in obedience to your Spirit; and, as you know our weakness, so may we know your power to save; through Jesus Christ our Lord. *Amen.*

Degol Stool *6 Genver*
A Dhuw Ollgalosek, a wrug hùmbronk dre gedyans an steren an dus fur dhe wordhya dha Vab, gwra gedya nacyons an nor der y wolow ev, may halla oll an bÿs meras orth dha glory; dre Jesu Crist agan Arlùth. *Amen.*

Degol Maria mis Whevrel *2 Whevrel*
A Das Ollgalosek, y feu dha Vab Jesu Crist presentys i'n Templa ha menegys dhe vos an glory a Israel ha golow an Jentylys, graunt dhyn ny rag y gerensa ev dhe vos presentys dhyragos rag may whrellen dastewynya y glory ev in oll an bÿs; dre Jesu Crist agan Arlùth. *Amen.*

Degol Maria mis Merth *25 Merth*
Ny a'th pës, a Arlùth, gwra devera dha râss aberth i'gan colon, ha kepar dell wrussyn clôwes a garnacyon dha Vab Jesu Crist dre vessach el, indella der y grows ha der y bassyon graunt may fen ny drës dhe glory y dhasserghyans, dre Jesu Crist agan Arlùth. *Amen.*

De Merher Lusow ha'n Corawys
A Dhuw Ollgalosek, may whrug dha Vab Jesu Crist penys i'n gwylfos dewgans dëdh hag y feu temptys kepar ha ny, heb pegh bytegyns; ro dhyn grâss dhe gesky agan honen in obedyens dhe'th Spyrys, ha kepar dell wodhesta agan gwander, indella graunt dhyn ny godhvos power brâs dha sylwans; dre Jesu Crist agan Arlùth. *Amen.*

Palm Sunday and Holy Week

Almighty and everlasting God, who of your tender love towards mankind, has sent your Son our Saviour Jesus Christ, to take upon him our flesh and to suffer death upon the cross, that all mankind should follow the example of his great humility; mercifully grant that we may both follow the example of his patience, and also be made partakers of his resurrection; through the same Jesus Christ our Lord. *Amen.*

Good Friday

Almighty God, we ask you graciously to look on this your family, for which our Lord Jesus Christ was content to be betrayed and given up into the hands of wicked men, and to suffer death upon the cross, who now lives and reigns with you and the Holy Spirit, ever one God, world without end. *Amen.*

Easter Day

Almighty God, who through your only Son Jesus Christ has overcome death and opened to us the gate of everlasting life: we humbly ask you to put into our minds good desires, so by your continual help, we may bring the same to good effect; through Jesus Christ our Lord. *Amen.*

Ascension Day until Pentecost

Grant we pray you, Almighty God, that as we do believe your only Son our Lord Jesus Christ to have ascended into the heavens, so we also in heart and mind may there ascend, and with him continually dwell, who lives and reigns with you and the Holy Spirit, one God, world without end. *Amen.*

De Sul Blejyow ha'n Seythen Sans

A Dhuw, a'th kerensa wheg tro ha mab den te a dhanvonas dha Vab agan Savyour Jesu Crist dhe gemeres warnodho agan kig ha godhevel mernans i'n growspren, rag may halla oll mebyon tus sewya patron y uvelder brâs; graunt dhyn a'th vercy indella dhe sewya ensompel y bassyon may fen ny kevrednek a'y dhasserghyans kefrÿs, der an keth Jesu Crist-ma agan Arlùth. *Amen.*

De Gwener an Grows

A Dhuw Ollgalosek, ny a'th pës a veras orth dha deylu jy, may feu agan Arlùth Jesu Crist pës dâ dhe vos traitys ragthans ha delyvrys inter dewla sherewys ha godhevel mernans i'n growspren, ev usy ow rainya yn few warbarth genes ha gans an Spyrys Sans, udn Duw bys venary, trank heb worfen. *Amen.*

Pask

A Dhuw Ollgalosek, dre dha Udn Vab Jesu Crist te re fethas mernans hag egery dhyn yettys an bêwnans dyvarow; yn uvel ny a'th pës dhe worra whansow dâ i'gan brës, may hallen ny dre dha weres heb fyllel dry in rag frûtys dâ anodhans; dre Jesu Crist agan Arlùth. *Amen.*

De Yow an Ascensyon bys Pencost

Graunt dhyn, ny a'th pës, a Dhuw Ollgalosek, kepar dell gresyn ny dha Un Vab dhe ascendya i'n nevow, may hallen nyny ascendya dy kefrÿs ha bos tregys ganso ev bys vycken, usy ow rainya yn few warbarth genes jy ha gans an Spyrys Sans trank heb worfen. *Amen.*

Pentecost (Whitsun)

God, who as at this time did teach the hearts of your faithful people by sending to them the light of your Holy Spirit; grant us by the same Spirit to have a right judgement in all things, and evermore to rejoice in his holy comfort; through the merits of Christ Jesus our Saviour, who lives and reigns with you in the unity of the same Spirit, one God, world without end. *Amen.*

Trinity Sunday

Almighty and everlasting God, who has given to us your servants grace by the confession of a true faith to acknowledge the glory of the eternal Trinity, and in the power of the Divine Majesty, to worship the unity: we ask that you may keep us steadfast in the faith, and evermore protect us from all adversities; who lives and reigns, one God, world without end. *Amen.*

The Birth of the Blessed Virgin Mary *8 September*

Almighty God, who chose the blessed Virgin Mary to be the mother of your only Son, grant that we who are redeemed by his blood may share with her in the glory of your eternal kingdom; through Jesus Christ our Lord. *Amen.*

All Saints' Day *1 November*

O Almighty God, who has knit together your elect in one communion and fellowship, in the mystical body of your Son Jesus Christ our Lord, grant us so to follow your blessed saints in all godly and virtuous living, that we may come to those unspeakable joys which you have prepared for those that truly love you; through Jesus Christ our Lord. *Amen.*

Pencost

A Dhuw, te a wrug desky avell i'n termyn-ma colonow dha bobel lel pan wrusta danvon dhedhans golow dha Spyrys Sans; graunt dhyn der an keth Spyrys-na dhe gafos brusyans ewn in kenyver tra ha dhe rejoycya benytha in y gonfort sans; dre veryt Jesu Crist agan Savyour, usy ow rainya yn few genes in ûnyta an keth Spyrys, udn Duw trank heb worfen. *Amen.*

De Sul an Drynsys

A Dhuw Ollgalosek nefra a bës, te re ros grâss dhe'th servysy dre veneges an grejyans wir dhe aswon glory an Drynsys dhyvarow, hag i'n gallos an Myternsys dewyl dhe wordhya an Ûnyta. Gwith ny yn fast y'n fëdh-ma may fen ny defendys nefra dhyworth pùb anken; dre Jesu Crist agan Arlùth, usy ow rainya yn few genes ha gans an Spyrys Sans, udn Duw trank heb worfen. *Amen.*

Genesygeth an Werhes Ker Maria *8 Gwyngala*

A Dhuw Ollgalosek, te a wrug dêwys an Werhes Ker Maria avell mabm a'th Udn Vab; graunt dhyn ny yw dasprenys der y woos dhe vos kevrednek gensy hy a'n glory a'th wlascor eternal; dre Jesu Crist agan Arlùth. *Amen.*

De Halan Gwâv *1 Du*

A Dhuw Ollgalosek, te a wrug gwia dha dus dêwysys warbarth in udn cowethyans ha company a'n corf mystycal a'th Vab Crist agan Arlùth; graunt dhyn indella dhe sewya dha Sens venegys in pùb vyrtu hag in bêwnans ewnhensek, may hallen ny dos bys i'n lowena-na na yll tavas derivas hag a wrusta parusy rag an re-na usy orth dha gara in gwir; dre Jesu Crist agan Arlùth. *Amen.*

St Winwaloe *3 March*

Almighty God, by whose grace the blessed abbot Winwaloe became a burning and shining light in your Church: kindle in us the same spirit of discipline and love, that we may ever walk before you as children of light; through Jesus Christ our Lord. *Amen.*

St Piran *5 March*

Almighty God, the light of the faithful and shepherd of souls, who brought your servant Piran to Cornwall's shores to feed your sheep by his word and guide them by his example: help us to keep the faith which he taught and to follow in his footsteps; through Jesus Christ our Lord. *Amen.*

St Michael, Protector of Cornwall *8 May*

Almighty God, we ask you to grant us your grace and send your strong servant Michael, the Blessed Archangel, bearing the bright sword of the spirit, to cleanse and protect our beloved land of Cornwall; through Jesus Christ our Lord. *Amen.*

St Petroc *4 June*

Almighty God, you enlightened Cornwall by the teaching of your servant Petroc. Enrich us evermore with your heavenly grace, and raise up faithful witnesses, who by their lives and teaching, may proclaim to all people the truth of your salvation; through Jesus Christ our Lord. *Amen.*

Dewydnek Sans *3 Merth*

A Dhuw Ollgalosek, yth esa Dewydnek an abas benegys golow ow lesky hag ow tewynya i'th Eglos: gwra anowy inon ny an keth spyrys a omrewl hag a gerensa, may hallen ny kerdhes dhyragos pùpprës avell flehes an golow; dre Jesu Crist agan Arlùth. *Amen.*

Peran Sans *5 Merth*

A Dhuw Ollgalosek, golow an re lel ha bugel an enevow, te a dhros dha servont Peran dhe gostys Kernow may halla va maga dha dheves der y eryow ha'ga gedya der y ensompel; gwra agan gweres ow sensy an fëdh a wruga desky dhyn ha dhe sewya olow y dreys; dre Jesu Crist agan Arlùth. *Amen.*

Myhal Arghel, Gwethyas Kernow *8 Me*

A Dhuw Ollgalosek, vossaw dhyn dha râss, ny a'th pës, ha danvon dhyn Myhal Arghel, dha servont benegys hag ev ow ton cledha spladn an Spyrys, may halla va glanhe yn tien hag gwetha orth kenyver drog agan tir ker Kernow; dre Grist agan Arlùth. *Amen.*

Petrok Sans *4 Metheven*

A Dhuw Ollgalosek, te a wrug golowy Kernow dre dhyscas dha servont Petrok. Gwra agan rychhe pupprys dre dha râss in mes a'n nev ha drehef in bàn dùstuniow lel, a alla der aga bêwnans ha der aga dyscas derivas dhe oll an bobel gwiryoneth dha salvacyon; dre Jesu Crist agan Arlùth. *Amen.*

Cornish Saints (men)

O God, who sent your servant *N* to be a master builder of your church in Cornwall, raise up, we pray, holy and faithful servants and labourers to build on the foundation he laid in our land; through Jesus Christ our Lord. *Amen.*

Cornish Saints (women)

O God, who sent your servant *N* to be a master builder of your church in Cornwall, raise up, we pray, holy and faithful servants and labourers to build on the foundation she laid in our land; through Jesus Christ our Lord. *Amen.*

A Martyr

Almighty God, by whose grace and power your holy martyr *N* triumphed over suffering and was faithful unto death; strengthen us with your grace that we may endure reproach and persecution, and faithfully bear witness to the name of Jesus Christ our Lord, in whose name we pray. *Amen.*

Any Saint

Almighty God, you have built your Church through the love and devotion of your saints; we give you thanks for your servant *N*, whom we commemorate today. Inspire us to follow his/her example, that we in our generation may rejoice with him/her in the vision of your glory; through Jesus Christ our Lord. *Amen.*

Sans a Gernow

A Dhuw, te a dhanvonas dha servont *N* dhe vos penser a'th eglos in Kernow, gwra dhe sevel in bàn, ny a'th pës, servysy hag oberoryon sans ha lel a wrella drehevel wàr an fùndacyon a veu settys ganso ev in hobma agan pow ny; dre Jesu Crist agan Arlùth. *Amen.*

Sanses a Gernow

A Dhuw, te a dhanvonas dha servyades *N* dhe vos penser a'th eglos in Kernow, gwra dhe sevel in bàn, ny a'th pës, servysy hag oberoryon sans ha lel a wrella drehevel wàr an fùndacyon a veu settys gensy hy in hobma agan pow ny; dre Jesu Crist agan Arlùth. *Amen.*

Merther

A Dhuw Ollgalosek, a wrug grâss ha nerth dhe'th verther/verthoryon sans *N* dhe gonqwerrya wàr bainys ha dhe vos lel bys in mernans; gwra agan nertha dre dha râss may hallen ny perthy rebuk ha compressans hag yn lel bos dùstuny rag hanow Jesu Crist agan Arlùth; usy ow rainya yn few genes ha gans an Spyrys Sans, udn Duw, lebmyn ha bys vycken. *Amen.*

Sans bò Sanses Vëth

A Dhuw Ollgalosek, te re formyas dha Eglos dre gerensa ha dre dhevocyon dha sens; yth eson ow ry dhis meur ras a'th servont *N*, uson ny ow remembra hedhyw. Gwra indella agan inia dhe sewya (h)y ensompel dâ, may hallen ny warbarth ganso ev/gensy hy rejoycya i'gan heneth ny ha gweles splander dha glory; dre Jesu Crist agan Arlùth. *Amen.*

Various Prayers

A Prayer for Cornwall
and the Cornish throughout the World

Almighty and most merciful Father, give your blessing, we pray you, to all Cornish people in this land and throughout the world, wherever they may be, whether in this island or across the seas, by land or by water, now and always. Bless the deeds and works of their hands and all that they undertake for Cornwall and for the world. Give them your aid to strengthen their hearts in their undertakings, thoughts, plans, crafts, art, and recreation of all kinds; and grant that they may do all things to your glory, in spirit and in truth, for the sake of our Lord Jesus Christ. *Amen.*

A Prayer for all Celtic peoples

Almighty God, Father of our Lord Jesus Christ, from whom every family in heaven and on earth is named, join, we pray you, in the bond of true brotherhood all the Celtic peoples, and by the power of your Holy Spirit guide their wills to use the great gifts they have been given to your glory, and that through them may be hastened your kingdom of peace and goodwill among men; through Jesus Christ our Lord. *Amen*

A Prayer for Cornishmen and women
who fell in conflict

Almighty God, we remember before you all those who through the ages have given their lives for Cornwall. Grant that following their examples we may never flinch from our duty however costly it may be. We ask this for the sake of him whose courage never failed, your only Son, our Saviour Jesus Christ. *Amen.*

Pejadow Dyvers

Pejadow rag Kernow
ha rag Kernowyon dres oll an Bÿs
A Das Ollgalosek leun a vercy, ny a'th pës a ry dha vedneth
i'n tor'-ma ha bys venary dhe bùb Kernow ha Kernowes
i'gan pow ny, i'n enys-ma ha dres oll an bÿs pynagoll le
may fons wàr an dor bò wàr an mor. Benyk obereth aga
dewla ha myns a wrellen rag les Kernow ha les oll an
norvÿs. Vossaw dhedhans dha nerth may halla va
confortya aga holon warlergh compas aga omgemeryans
in preder, towl, creft, lien bò gwary kyn fe, ha graunt
dhedhans oll dha wordhya jy in spyrys hag in gwiryoneth
dre râss agan Arlùth Jesu Crist. *Amen.*

Pejadow rag oll an poblow Keltek
A Dhuw Ollgalosek, Tas agan Arlùth Jesu Crist, ahanas jy
yma henwys pùb teylu i'n nev hag i'n nor, ny a'th pës a
gelmy warbarth in cowethas a vredereth ha lendury oll an
Poblow Keltek, ha graunt dhedhans dre vyrtu dha Spyrys
Sans dhe ûsya an royow a ressys dhedhans rag may hallens
wordhya yn compes ha spedya dha wlascor a râss hag a
volùnjeth dâ inter oll an nacyons; dre Jesu Crist agan
Arlùth. *Amen.*

Pejadow rag remembra Kernowyon
a godhas yn batel
A Dhuw Ollgalosek, yth eson ny ow remembra dhyragos
oll an re-na der an osow a ros aga bêwnans rag Kernow.
Graunt ny indella dhe sewya aga ensompel dâ ma na
wrellen ny nefra forsakya agan dûta, costyens a gostya. Ny
a bës hebma rag y gerensa ev na wrug y golonecter
bythqueth fyllel, dha Udn Vab, agan Savyour Jesu Crist.
Amen.

A Prayer of Penitence

Almighty God, our Heavenly Father, we have sinned against you through our own fault, in thought and word and deed, and in what we have left undone. We are heartily sorry, and repent of all our sins. For your Son our Lord Jesus Christ's sake, forgive us all that is past, and grant that we may serve you in newness of life, to the glory of your name. *Amen.*

A Morning Prayer

O Lord our Heavenly Father, Almighty and Everlasting God, who has brought us safely to the beginning of this day. Protect us in the same with your mighty power and grant that today we fall into no sin, nor run into any kind of danger; but grant that all our deeds may be ordered by your rule, so we may always do what is righteous in your sight; through Jesus Christ our Lord. *Amen.*

An Evening Prayer

Lighten our darkness, Lord, we pray, and in your great mercy defend us from all perils and dangers of this night, for the love of your only Son, Jesus Christ our Lord. *Amen.*

A Blessing

The peace of God which passes all understanding, keep our hearts and minds in the knowledge and love of God, and of his Son, Jesus Christ; and the blessing of God Almighty, the Father, the Son and the Holy Spirit, be with us and remain with us always. *Amen.*

Pejadow Penytens

A Dhuw Ollgalosek, agan Tas a nev, ny re behas wàr dha bydn jy der agan camhenseth agan honen, in preder, in ger hag in gwrians hag i'n taclow kefrÿs a wrussyn gasa heb aga gul. Casadow dhyn yw agan pehosow hag edreg tydn a'gan beus anodhans. Gav dhyn rag kerensa dha Vab agan Arlùth Jesu Crist pùptra eus passyes ha graunt dhyn may hallen dha servya dre vêwnans nowyth alebma rag may fe gordhyes dha hanow jy. *Amen.*

Pejadow Myttyn

A Arlùth agan Tas in nev, a Dhuw Ollgalosek ha dyvarow, te re'gan dros yn saw dhe dhalleth an jorna-ma. Gwra agan dyffres i'n keth dëdh-ma der dha bower galosek ha vossaw hedhyw na wrellen ny codha in pegh vëth naneyl resek in peryl a sort vëth oll; mes graunt dh'agan oberow bos indella ordnys dre dha rewlyans may hallen ny gul pùpprës an pëth a vo ewn i'th wolok jy; dre Jesu Crist agan Arlùth. *Amen.*

Pejadow Gordhuwher

Gwra golowy agan tewolgow, ny a'th pës a Arlùth; ha dre dha vercy brâs gwra agan defendya dhyworth pùb peryl ha danjer a'n nos-ma; rag kerensa dha Udn Vab, agan Savyour Jesu Crist. *Amen.*

Bedneth

Cres Duw usy ow passya pùb convedhes, re wetho agan colon ha brës i'n godhvos hag i'n gerensa a Dhuw ha'y Vab Jesu Crist agan Arlùth; ha re bo genen bedneth Duw Ollgalosek an Tas, an Mab ha'n Spyrys Sans ha re wrello trega genen benytha. *Amen.*

Commemorating our Celtic Saints and Martyrs

At the beginning of the ninth century when the Church in Cornwall was already nearly 700 years old, it was not under the control of either the Anglo-Saxon Archbishop of Canterbury or the Pope in Rome, yet it was in communion with both. This Cornish Church was part of the original Celtic Church established in these isles centuries before the first missionaries arrived from Rome in 597 AD.

The Celtic Church was renowned for its holiness, tolerance and lack of the legalistic and destructive authoritarianism often seen in the Anglo-Saxon and Roman Churches. There is no record of the Celtic Church ever persecuting or oppressing anyone. It had a strong sense of the presence of God in the world and a deep respect for his creation. Women had virtual equal status with men and often held positions of authority over them. Power, status and influence in this Church depended on personal holiness, not on one's gender or position in a hierarchy of authority. People withdrew from society to deepen their faith. Brave Celtic monks and nuns travelled hundreds of miles across dangerous seas to spread the Gospel in leaky coracles made of sticks and hides, crossing Cornwall by travelling up or down the Hayle, Fowey, or Camel estuaries to avoid the dangerous currents and rocks around Land's End.

This golden age of the Celtic Saints in Cornwall ended when the Church in Canterbury assumed control over the Cornish Church in the wake of the Anglo-Saxon military assault on Cornwall in 838 AD. Since then, the distinctiveness of the Church in Cornwall has been eroded away until it is now indistinguishable from that in England. Many today mourn for the lost ethos of the Celtic Church and see regaining its attractive qualities as the key to the spiritual renewal of our Cornish Church. Perhaps this little book will help you restore a little of this ethos whenever you use it, wherever you are.

Below is a list of the holy days of the more important Celtic saints of this era and of Cornwall, including a short pen-picture of each. Only those Cornish saints we have some reliable information about have been included—it would be difficult seeking to commemorate those of whom we know nothing or only fantastic fables.

This list is to supplement a standard lectionary, so you can draw inspiration from those who founded and built up the Celtic Church by remembering them in prayer on their particular day. The brave Cornishmen and women who sacrificed their lives in defence of our national and religious freedoms have also been included, because our debt to them is as great.

To all Celtic saints and martyrs, ancient, old and new, be praise, glory and honour now and for all eternity. *Amen.*

St Bridget *1 February*

A vivacious, kind nun who was converted and baptized by St Patrick, she went onto become his successor and the most important Irish saint after him, founding many convents and monasteries, and choosing those she thought worthy to be consecrated bishop. Like him, she is now venerated throughout Ireland and the Irish Diaspora and was granted the honour of being buried beside him.

St Ia *3 February*

The daughter of an Irish chieftain, she came to evangelise Cornwall with St Gwinear. She landed at Hayle, luckily avoiding martyrdom by King Tewdrig. The town of St Ives is named after her.

St David, Patron of Wales *1 March*

Very little is known about St David, except he was born of royal blood about 530, was taught and ordained by St Illtud, and then became Bishop of Menevia (now called St David's). Judging by the amount of legends about him and church dedications, he was a most revered and saintly bishop who founded many monasteries and convents before his death in about 589.

St Winwaloe of Landévennec *3 March*

Born of a Cornish refugee family at St Brieuc in Brittany in the fifth century, Winwaloe trained as a monk under St Budoc before attempting to found a monastery on the island of Tibidy. However, its infertile soil and high winds compelled Winwaloe to seek more favourable conditions, which he found on the coast of western Brittany at Landévennec. There he established an extremely important monastery, his monks living under the most austere of rules. He died in about 532, and is regarded today as one of the seven most important saints of Brittany, the site of his monastery now being inhabited by monks of the Benedictine Order. He may well have visited Cornwall at some time as there are a number of churches there dedicated to him.

St Piran, Patron of Cornwall *5 March*

Little is known too about the historical St Piran as the *Life of Piran* that bears his name is an adaptation of the *Life of Ciaran*, another saint. It seems he was a Welshman who made the traditional missionary journey to Cornwall, landing near Perranporth. His ancient oratory lies buried in the sands nearby, but his stone cross can still be clearly seen. He then went onto continue his work in Brittany where he is also venerated and where other villages and churches are dedicated to his name.

St Constantine *9 March*

A Cornish king converted by St Petroc, he abdicated in favour of his son when his beloved wife died and went off to become a monk in Ireland. He then went to Scotland where he became its first Christian martyr.

St Paul Aurelian *12 March*

Known in Brittany as St Pol de Leon, he was the son of a Welsh chieftain. He became a monk and trained with St David and St Samson under St Illtud before setting off for Cornwall. He met his sister in Mount's Bay and helped establish her convent above Newlyn where the village and church of Paul still bear his name. He went onto become Bishop of Leon in Brittany and one of its most venerated saints.

St Patrick, Patron and Apostle of Ireland *17 March*

Born of Christian parents near Dumbarton in 387, he was carried off into slavery when 16 years old by Irish raiders and sold to a chieftain in present day Co. Antrim, Ireland. He spent six years as a shepherd in the fields where he grew closer and closer to God despite druidic influences around him. He fled to Britain before leaving for Gaul to be taught by St Germanus of Auxerre. Germanus then sent him to Rome to meet the Pope. In about 433, Patrick was sent back to Ireland, where he was to eventually wrestle its people from the control of the druids, firmly establishing the Christian faith there. He died on this day in 493, and was buried under the Cathedral of Down.

St Gwinear *23 March*

A sixth-century Irish martyr, who landed in the Hayle estuary, intending to convert the Cornish. He was promptly killed by King Tewdrig along with many of his followers, but fortunately saints Ia and Erc survived.

St Goran *7 April*

A hermit who lived on Rough Tor on Bodmin Moor, he gave St Petroc shelter when he first moved there from Padstow. The ruins of St Goran's little cell can still be found there. Having helped St Petroc get established, St Goran humbly bowed out and settled two miles south of Mevagissey in the village which still bears his name.

St Endellion *29 April*

A daughter of King Brychan, she left Wales for Cornwall in search of a solitary life of prayer. She lived at Tretinny just half a mile from St Endellion, and quickly became renowned as a holy and kind woman. She lived a very simple life, drinking only the milk from her single cow. When she was old and lay dying, Endellion asked her friends to put her body on a sledge and to let it be pulled by two oxen. Wherever they chose to stop was where she wanted to be buried. They stopped on top of a marshy hill not far away where St Endellion Church stands today.

St Buriana *1 May*

The daughter of an Irish chieftain, she came to Cornwall in the fifth century and established an important religious house at St Buryan. King Athelstan of England visited it in the tenth century. He was so impressed, he endowed it and paid for a church to be built there. Unfortunately, he also forced it and other Cornish monasteries to be reformed, and their Celtic character was lost as a result.

St Michael, Protector of Cornwall *8 May*

One of the three archangels of the Christian Church, he is reputed to have appeared on Mount Gargano in Italy on 8 May 492. As a result, he is associated with high places such as St Michael's Mount and Glastonbury Tor (whose church was dedicated to him), and he is patron of many churches throughout Cornwall. It is thought he may be a Christianized Celtic messenger god, which might explain his popularity. His title of Protector of Cornwall may have arisen when Robert, Count of Mortain and Duke of Cornwall, wore the emblem of St Michael in battle in the eleventh century.

St Carantoc *16 May*

Ordained in Wales, he left for Ireland where he assisted St Patrick, founding many churches and monasteries. In about 520, he returned to Wales and went onto Cornwall with St Enoder to continue his work. There is a Holy Well near Crantock dedicated to his name. He eventually went to Brittany where he is also venerated.

St Petroc of Cornwall *4 June*

The son of a Welsh king, he renounced any claims to his father's throne, became a monk, and went to Ireland to study. There he taught one of its most famous saints, St Kevin, before leaving for Cornwall. He landed in the Camel estuary and founded a monastery at Padstow. After many years, he moved inland and founded another monastery at Bodmin. He died and was buried in Padstow. The empty ivory casket that used to contain his bones can still be seen in St Petroc's Church, Bodmin. The remains of his oratory are nearby.

St Meriasek *7 June*

A sixth-century bishop who probably landed at Hayle with St Gwinear. He went onto become Bishop of Vannes in Brittany. A play (*Bewnans Meryasek*) was written about him in Cornish.

St Columba of Iona, Apostle of the Scots *9 June*

Born in 521 in Co Donegal, Ireland, he was ordained Priest at the monastery at Clonard. Having become involved in a bloody clan war, Columba was struck with remorse. In confession afterwards, he was given the penance of preaching the Gospel in Britain. He left Ireland and founded the important monastery of Iona in Scotland in 563 from where Scotland and Northumbria were evangelized. After spending many years converting the Scots of the Kingdom of Dalriada, he then devoted the rest of his life to preaching the Gospel to the Picts of Northern Scotland. He died at Iona in 597, the year the first mission from Rome arrived in Canterbury led by St Augustine.

St Nectan *17 June*
The eldest son of a Welsh king, he first lived in Devon before probably moving to the Tintagel area. Nearby is St Nectan's Glen with a waterfall he is reputably buried under. He tried to convert two robbers to Christianity who were trying to steal his cows. He was martyred when they beheaded him.

The Cornish Martyrs of 1497 *27 June*
In 1497, King Henry VII sought to impose taxation upon Cornwall in order to raise money for an army to invade Scotland. A Bodmin lawyer, Thomas Flamank, argued the tax was illegal, and recognized the threat to Cornwall's constitutional status, freedom and rights. He joined forces with Joseph An Gof, a charismatic blacksmith from St Keverne, and they led a deputation to London, demanding that the King think again. On 17 June, the Cornish were attacked at Blackheath by the King's forces. Flamank and An Gof were captured, and hung, drawn and quartered ten days later. An Gof defiantly proclaimed before he died that he would "have a name perpetual, a fame permanent and immortal." In Cornwall, he and Flamank always shall.

St Samson *28 July*

The son of a Welsh chieftain born about 490 in South Wales, he became a monk, was taught and ordained by St Illtud, and became abbot of Caldey Island. He then travelled to Ireland where he was accredited with many miracles. He was made bishop somewhere on the North Devon coast before moving down to central Cornwall where Golant Church is still dedicated to his name. He left to become a pillar of the Breton church and Bishop of Dol in about 520, where he eventually died in about 565.

St Neot *31 July*

Neot was a monk at Glastonbury Abbey who decided he wanted to live as a hermit in Cornwall and built his monastic cell and church at St Neot. Neot was very short—so short he needed to stand on a stool when saying mass. Neot lived a holy life before his death and burial in St Neot's Church, his bones later being taken away to become places of pilgrimage in England. However, Neot will always be commemorated in Cornwall in the Medieval stained glass windows in St Neot's church, depicting scenes from his life. The holy well in which he used to pray is nearby.

The Cornish Martyrs of 1549 *4 August*
In 1534, Henry VIII abolished the Pope's authority in his realm and established the Church of England under his own rule. In 1549, his Archbishop of Canterbury, Thomas Cranmer, sought to impose his new English language prayer book on Cornwall, and to end many ancient religious traditions and practices. The people of Cornwall rose under the leadership of Sir Humphrey Arundell in defence of their language and their civil right to worship as they wished. Not wanting to parley, the King's forces met Cornwall's near Exeter, defeated them, and on this day slaughtered all 900 of their Cornish prisoners. It is thought at least a tenth of Cornwall's population was massacred in the retribution that followed. Many people in Cornwall have only recently become aware of this shocking historical event, the consequences of which are arguably still felt in Cornwall today.

St Aidan, Apostle of Northumbria *31 August*
An Irish monk who became Bishop of Clogher and then went to Iona in about 630. King Oswald of Northumbria sent a request there for Christian monks to come and found a monastery on the Holy Island of Lindisfarne. Such was Aidan's holiness, he was chosen to be its first Bishop and arrived there in 634. He became firm friends with King Oswald, and was renowned for his learning, eloquent preaching, holiness and humility. Under his and his successor St Cuthbert's wise rule, Lindisfarne became the centre of learning and Christian mission for all of northern England. He died in 651 at Bamborough Castle.

St Ninian, Apostle of the Picts *16 September*
The eighth-century historian, the Venerable Bede, wrote
"the southern Picts received the true faith by the
preaching of Bishop Ninias, a most revered and holy man
of the British nation." St Ninian founded an important
monastery at Whithorn, near Stranraer, where Scotland
was evangelized from and where he was buried in about
432.

St Kea *3 October*
Born of noble parents somewhere in Britain, Kea became
a priest and then a bishop. He sold all he had to support
the poor, but, feeling weighed down by his responsibilities,
he went to Wales to live as a hermit. Kea then journeyed
to Old Kea on the Roseland Peninsula in Cornwall. He
later sailed for Brittany and established a monastery there
at Cléder. Kea was to return to Britain, hoping to stop a
war between Arthur and Mordred to claim the British
crown. Failing to do so, Kea returned to Brittany to
Cléder, where he died and was buried.

St Erc *31 October*
Converted and then consecrated Bishop of Slane by St
Patrick. The brother of St Ia, he was one of a group of Irish
missionaries who landed in the Hayle estuary with St
Gwinear. The nearby village of St Erth is named after him.

St Winnoc *6 November*
A Welshman who came to Cornwall and established a church on the River Fowey where a church is still named after him. He went onto Brittany and then to found a monastery near Dunkirk in about 700 with two Celtic colleagues. After his death in 715, his shrine was to become a major place of continental pilgrimage.

St Illtud of Wales *6 November*
Reputably the son of a Breton prince born about 480, his father hoped he would become a monk, but Illtud chose the military life instead. He went to Wales in search of adventure, and was nearly killed after falling in a bog. As a result, he returned to the faith and, after monastic training, he founded the important Welsh monastery at Llanilltud Fawr, which was to act as the powerhouse of monasticism for the Celtic world for many years. Probably the most important and learned Welsh saint, he taught and ordained many others such as David, Samson and Paul Aurelian. He may have returned to Brittany shortly before his death.

St Cuby *8 November*
A Cornishman of royal blood possibly born at Cuby, he refused the crown so he might become a monk. He followed in the traditions of the missionary Celtic saints, but travelled in the opposite direction. He went to Ireland and then to Wales where he has been called "one of the makers of Christian Wales." He founded an important monastery on Holy Island, Anglesea.

St Columb *13 November*
A Christian nun and disciple of St Carantoc who resisted and fled the advances of a pagan admirer. He then pursued and beheaded her at Ruthvos (*red wall* in Cornish) near St Columb Major when she refused to renounce her faith.

St Hilda of Whitby *17 November*
Born in 614 in Northumbria, she was asked to found a combined monastery and nunnery at Hartlepool by St Aiden in the manner established by St Bridget. It was a great success, and she went onto establish and rule an even more important joint monastery and convent at Whitby. It was there that the pivotal Synod of Whitby was held in 664 at which she was present, and where she defended the traditions and practices of the Celtic Church against the criticism of the Anglo-Saxon Church in Canterbury. The Celts lost, and the church in Northumbria came under Canterbury's control and had to conform to its ways.

St Budoc *8 December*
His Breton mother was driven out to sea by her enemies. She gave birth there to St Budoc before landing in Ireland. He grew up and was educated there and became a monk. He was sent to Wales and eventually reached Cornwall where he founded a church at the village near Falmouth which, with its church, still bears his name.

Rules of the Church's Year

If you do not have a lectionary of the Church's year, the following rules will help you determine when to keep certain days and when Advent and Lent, the periods of spiritual preparation for Christmas and Easter, begin and end:

Advent begins on Advent Sunday and is the fourth Sunday before Christmas.

The Epiphany is celebrated on the sixth of January.

Ash Wednesday is the first day of Lent and falls in the seventh week before Easter.

Lent ends with Palm Sunday, which is the Sunday before Easter.

Ascension Day is on a Thursday forty days after Easter Day.

Pentecost (Whit Sunday) is the second Sunday after Ascension Day.

Trinity Sunday is the Sunday after Pentecost.

Acknowledgements

This book has been sponsored by *Cowethas Peran Sans*, the Fellowship of St Piran. *Cowethas Peran Sans* is an ecumenical Cornish Christian fellowship whose members seek to understand and embody the spirituality of Cornwall's Celtic Saints, to share this spirituality with others, and to walk more gently upon this fragile earth. *Cowethas Peran Sans* seeks to promote use of the Cornish language in prayer and worship, but does not support any one particular orthography of Cornish over and above others. You can find out more about *Cowethas Peran Sans* by visiting our website at *www.peran.org.uk*.

Cowethas Peran Sans would like to thank Professor Nicholas Williams for his work in translation and Michael Everson for typesetting and publishing this book, which was conceived and compiled by Andy Phillips.